FIRST SOLOS

from the Classics

*for the violin in the
first position with
piano accompaniment*

by SAMUEL APPLEBAUM

Ed. 2160

ISBN 978-0-7935-4530-8

G. SCHIRMER, Inc.

DISTRIBUTED BY

HAL•LEONARD®
CORPORATION
7777 W. BLUEMOUND RD. P.O. BOX 13819 MILWAUKEE, WI 53213

Foreword

This collection represents a minimum number of pieces to be studied in the first position. They are ideally suited for recital and study purposes. They may be followed by "Master-Works for the Young Violinist" arranged by Samuel Applebaum and Eric Steiner.

A dot over or under a note refers to the martelé stroke. A dash over or under a note refers to the smooth détaché stroke.

The small notes are to be stopped by the fingers but not played. This anticipatory fingering is a valuable aid to the development of a good left-hand technique. The lines indicate that the fingers are to remain on the string.

The measures are numbered according to phrases and sections. Study the placement of these numbers for a structural analysis of each piece. This is beneficial not only from the standpoint of good musicianship, but as an aid to memorizing. Watch for phrases that begin on an up-beat or in the middle of a measure.

SAMUEL APPLEBAUM

Index by Composers

Index by Title

Barcarolle

from "The Tales of Hoffmann"

Jacques Offenbach
Transcribed by Samuel Applebaum

Soldiers' March

Robert Schumann, Op. 68, No. 2
Transcribed by Samuel Applebaum

Air

Ballet Music from "Orpheus"

C. W. von Gluck
Transcribed by Samuel Applebaum

Melody in F

Anton Rubinstein, Op.3
Transcribed by Samuel Applebaum

Country Gardens

English Morris Dance
Transcribed by Samuel Applebaum

Melody in F

Anton Rubinstein, Op.3
Transcribed by Samuel Applebaum

Waltz

Johannes Brahms, Op.39
Transcribed by Samuel Applebaum

Come Let Us to the Bagpipes Sound

from the Peasant Cantata

Johann Sebastian Bach
Transcribed by Samuel Applebaum

17

Gavotte
from the Fifth French Suite

Johann Sebastian Bach
Transcribed by Samuel Applebaum

*The new phrase will begin on the third beat of the fourth measure.

Copyright, MCMLIV, by G. Schirmer, Inc.

Träumerei
Reverie

Robert Schumann, Op. 15, No. 7
Transcribed by Samuel Applebaum

FIRST SOLOS
from the Classics

by SAMUEL APPLEBAUM

Index by Title

ISBN 978-0-7935-4530-8

G. SCHIRMER, Inc.

DISTRIBUTED BY

HAL•LEONARD®
CORPORATION
7777 W. BLUEMOUND RD. P.O. BOX 13819 MILWAUKEE, WI 53213

Barcarolle
from "The Tales of Hoffmann"

Violin

Jacques Offenbach
Transcribed by Samuel Applebaum

Soldiers' March

Violin

Robert Schumann, Op. 68, No. 2
Transcribed by Samuel Applebaum

Air

Ballet Music from "Orpheus"

Violin

C. W. von Gluck
Transcribed by Samuel Applebaum

Melody in F

Violin

Anton Rubinstein, Op.3
Transcribed by Samuel Applebaum

5

Country Gardens

Violin

English Morris Dance
Transcribed by Samuel Applebaum

Waltz

Violin

Johannes Brahms, Op. 39
Transcribed by Samuel Applebaum

Come Let Us to the Bagpipes Sound

from the Peasant Cantata

Johann Sebastian Bach
Transcribed by Samuel Applebaum

Violin

Gavotte
from the Fifth French Suite

Violin

Johann Sebastian Bach
Transcribed by Samuel Applebaum

*The new phrase will begin on the third beat of the fourth measure.

Träumerei

Reverie

Violin

Robert Schumann, Op. 15, No. 7
Transcribed by Samuel Applebaum

See, the Conquering Hero Comes

from "Judas Maccabaeus"

Violin

George Frideric Handel
Transcribed by Samuel Applebaum

Watchman's Song

Inspired by a performance of Shakespeare's Macbeth

Violin

Edvard Grieg, Op. 12, No. 3
Transcribed by Samuel Applebaum

Minuet in C

Violin

Wolfgang Amadeus Mozart, K.439b
Transcribed by Samuel Applebaum

*In passages like these, the dot indicates that the note is to be shortened — as though it were an 8th note followed by an 8th rest.

Amaryllis
Air de Louis XIII

Violin

Henri Ghys, Op. 10, No. 2
Transcribed by Samuel Applebaum

Allegro moderato

*Use the détaché or spiccato strokes on notes with the dot and dash

Andante

from Surprise Symphony

Violin

Joseph Haydn
Transcribed by Samuel Applebaum

Waves of the Danube

Violin

G. Ivanovici
Transcribed by Samuel Applebaum

Minuet in A

Violin

Wolfgang Amadeus Mozart, K.439b
Transcribed by Samuel Applebaum

Trumpeter's Serenade

Violin

Fritz Spindler, Op. 249, No. 20
Transcribed by Samuel Applebaum

*Use the spiccato bowing for the 8th notes with dots and the martelé bowing for the 8th notes followed by 8th rests.

See, the Conquering Hero Comes

from "Judes Maccabaeus'

George Frideric Handel
Transcribed by Samuel Applebaum

22

Watchman's Song

Inspired by a performance of Shakespeare's Macbeth

Edvard Grieg, Op. 12, No.3
Transcribed by Samuel Applebaum

Minuet in C

Wolfgang Amadeus Mozart, K. 439b
Transcribed by Samuel Applebaum

Minuet D.C.

Amaryllis
Air de Louis XIII

Henri Ghys, Op. 10, No. 2
Transcribed by Samuel Applebaum

Andante
from Surprise Symphony

Joseph Haydn
Transcribed by Samuel Applebaum

Waves of the Danube

G. Ivanovici
Transcribed by Samuel Applebaum

Minuet in A

Wolfgang Amadeus Mozart, K.439b
Transcribed by Samuel Applebaum

Trumpeter's Serenade

Fritz Spindler, Op. 249, No. 20
Transcribed by Samuel Applebaum